Take Care of Yourself

Looking After Your Teeth

Siân Smith

www.raintreepublishers.co.uk
Visit our website to find out more information about Raintree books.

To order:
☎ Phone 0845 6044371
🖹 Fax +44 (0) 1865 312263
✉ Email myorders@raintreepublishers.co.uk

Customers from outside the UK please telephone +44 1865 312262

Raintree is an imprint of Capstone Global Library Limited, a company incorporated in England and Wales having its registered office at 7 Pilgrim Street, London, EC4V 6LB– Registered company number: 6695582

Edited by Dan Nunn, Rebecca Rissman, and John-Paul Wilkins
Designed by Victoria Allen
Picture research by Tracy Cummins
Production by Alison Parsons
Originated by Capstone Global Library Ltd
Printed and bound in China by Leo Paper Products Ltd

ISBN 978 1 406 24158 7
16 15 14 13 12
10 9 8 7 6 5 4 3 2 1

British Library Cataloguing in Publication Data
Smith, Siân.
Looking after your teeth. – (Take care of yourself)
617.6'01-dc22
A full catalogue record for this book is available from the British Library.

Acknowledgements
We would like to thank the following for permission to reproduce photographs: Capstone Library pp. 9, 12, 13, 23c (Karon Dubke); Getty Images pp. 7 (Marilyn Conway), 8 (Peter Cade), 14 right (Tom Grill), 17, 20, 23a (Image Source), 19 (ERproductions Ltd), 22 (Tom Grill); istockphoto pp. 14 left (© Kim Gunkel), 21 (© Richard Hydren); Shutterstock pp. 4 (© Vladimir Wrangel), 5 (© Monkey Business Images), 6, 23b (© Levent Konuk), 10 (© Gemenacom), 11 (© ilFede), 15 (© Alexander Trinitatov), 146 (© Jaimie Duplass), 18 (© Andreas Gradin).

Front cover photograph of girl brushing teeth reproduced with permission of Getty Images (Blend Images). Rear cover photograph of funny young girl eating corn reproduced with permission of Shutterstock (© ladimir Wrangel).

Every effort has been made to contact copyright holders of material reproduced in this book. Any omissions will be rectified in subsequent printings if notice is given to the publisher.

We would like to thank Nesha Patel, Nancy Harris, and Dee Reid for their assistance in the preparation of this book.

Contents

Why should I look after my teeth?

You need your teeth to eat food.

Your teeth get plaque on them after you eat.

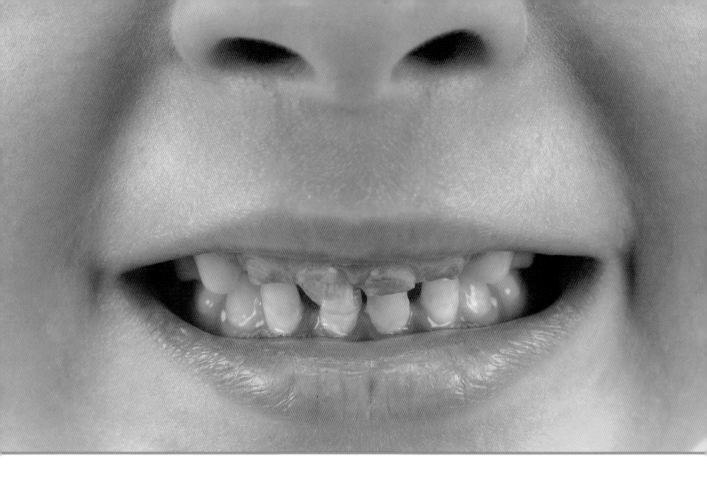

Plaque makes teeth go bad.

This makes your teeth hurt.

How to brush your teeth

When you brush your teeth
you get rid of the plaque.

Put a pea-sized bit of toothpaste on your brush.

Brush around every tooth.

Brush the hard to reach
places, too.

timer

Brush for about two minutes.
You could use a timer to help you.

Spit the toothpaste out in the sink.

When should I brush my teeth?

Brush your teeth after breakfast.

Brush your teeth before you sleep.

Brush your teeth after lunch
or snacks if you can.

Other ways to look after your teeth

You can drink water at any time.

Water is not bad for your teeth.

Sweets are bad for your teeth.
Sugary drinks are bad for your teeth.

Try not to have sweet things
very often.

Brush your teeth afterwards
if you can.

You should see the dentist twice a year.

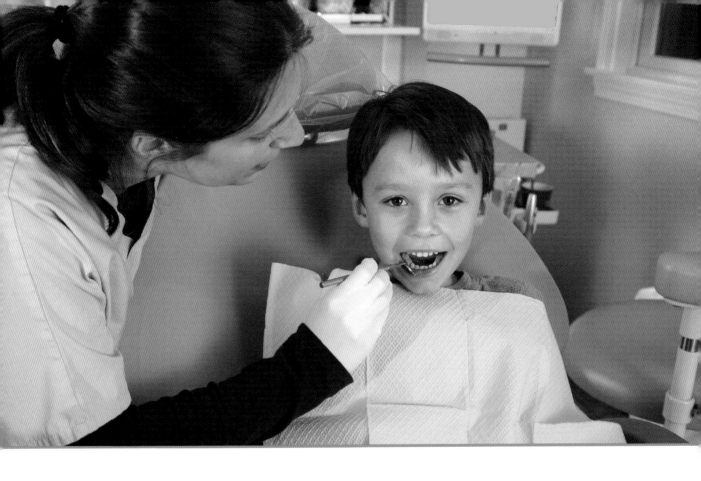

The dentist will check to see if your
teeth are clean and healthy.

Can you remember?

When should you brush your teeth?

Answer on page 24

Picture glossary

 **dentist** doctor who looks after people's teeth

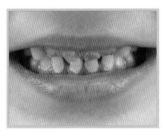 **plaque** something you get on your teeth after you eat or drink. You cannot see plaque but it is bad for your teeth.

 **timer** machine a bit like a clock. A timer can tell you how long it takes to do something.

Index

Answer to question on page 22
You need to brush your teeth after breakfast and before you go to bed.
You should also brush your teeth after eating lunch, snacks, or sweet things if you can.

Notes for parents and teachers
Before reading
Ask the children why we need teeth. Find out what they know about how to take care of their teeth and record their ideas. Read the book to see where these ideas overlap.

After reading
- If possible, ask a dentist or hygienist to speak to the children about what they need to do to take care of their teeth. Use a toothbrush, model of teeth, and a timer and ask a child to brush the teeth for 2 minutes. Which teeth were harder to clean? Demonstrate how to brush your teeth well.
- Draw a face with an open, smiling mouth (crescent shaped). Give the children a quiz on how to look after their teeth. For each question they get right add a tooth to the mouth. Can they collect a full set of teeth?